First World War
and Army of Occupation
War Diary
France, Belgium and Germany

1 DIVISION
3 Infantry Brigade
Royal Welsh Fusiliers
4 Battalion
5 November 1914 - 31 August 1915

WO95/1280/2

The Naval & Military Press Ltd
www.nmarchive.com
Published in association with The National Archives

Published by

The Naval & Military Press Ltd

Unit 10 Ridgewood Industrial Park,

Uckfield, East Sussex,

TN22 5QE England

Tel: +44 (0) 1825 749494

www.naval-military-press.com

www.nmarchive.com

This diary has been reprinted in facsimile from the original. Any imperfections are inevitably reproduced and the quality may fall short of modern type and cartographic standards.

© **Crown Copyright**
Images reproduced by permission of The National Archives, London, England, 2015.

Contents

Document type	Place/Title	Date From	Date To
Heading	1Div 3 Infantry Brig WO95 1280/2 4 Bttn Royal Welsh Fusiliers		
Heading	1st Division 3rd Infantry Brigade. 4th Battalion Royal Welsh Fusiliers 1914 Nov-1915 Aug. To 47 Div (Pioneers)		
Heading	1st Division 3rd Brigade 4th Battalion Royal Welsh Fusiliers Jan-Aug 1915		
Heading	File with 3rd Brigade. 1st Division. Battalion disembarked Havre 6.11.14. Joined 3rd Brigade 6th December 1914. 4th Battalion Royal Welsh Fusiliers. November 1914		
War Diary	Northampton	05/11/1914	05/11/1914
War Diary	Le Havre	06/11/1914	06/11/1914
War Diary	Bleville Camp	07/11/1914	07/11/1914
War Diary	Bleville	07/11/1914	08/11/1914
War Diary	Haure	08/11/1914	08/11/1914
War Diary	Journey to Paint Omer	09/11/1914	09/11/1914
War Diary	St Omer	10/11/1914	11/11/1914
War Diary	Heuringhem	11/11/1914	01/12/1914
Heading	3rd Brigade. 1st Division. Battalion joined 3rd Brigade from L of C. 7th December '14. 4th Battalion Royal Welsh Fusiliers December 1914		
War Diary	Heuringhem	01/12/1914	05/12/1914
War Diary	Heuringhem to Hazebrouck	06/12/1914	06/12/1914
War Diary	Hazebrouck to Bailleul	07/12/1914	07/12/1914
War Diary	Bailleul	08/12/1914	20/12/1914
War Diary	Merville to Bethune	21/12/1914	21/12/1914
War Diary	Festubert	22/12/1914	01/01/1915
Heading	1st Division 3rd Brigade. War Diary 4th Royal Welsh Fusiliers January 1915		
War Diary		01/01/1915	01/01/1915
War Diary	Festubert	02/01/1915	05/01/1915
War Diary	Bethune	09/01/1915	14/01/1915
War Diary	Givenchy	15/01/1915	31/01/1915
Heading	1st Division 3rd Brigade. War Diary 4th Royal Welsh Fusiliers February 1915		
War Diary	Givenchy	01/02/1915	03/02/1915
War Diary	Marles-le-Mines	04/02/1915	25/02/1915
War Diary	Essars	26/01/1915	28/02/1915
Heading	1st Division 3rd Brigade. War Diary 4th Royal Welch Fusiliers March 1915		
War Diary	Essars	01/03/1915	06/03/1915
War Diary	Festubert	07/03/1915	31/03/1915
Heading	3rd Infantry Brigade. 1st Division. War Diary 4th Battn. Royal Welsh Fusiliers April 1915		
War Diary	Neuve Chapelle	01/04/1915	07/04/1915
War Diary	Les. Choques	08/04/1915	14/04/1915
War Diary	Rue-de-L'E Pinette	15/04/1915	24/04/1915
War Diary	Harisoirs	25/04/1915	30/04/1915

Heading	3rd Infantry Brigade. 1st Division. War Diary 4th Battn. Royal Welsh Fusiliers May 1915		
War Diary	Harisoirs	01/05/1915	06/05/1915
War Diary	Hinges	07/05/1915	08/05/1915
War Diary	Rue-de-Bois	09/05/1915	09/05/1915
War Diary	Harisoir	10/05/1915	10/05/1915
War Diary	Long Cornet	11/05/1915	11/05/1915
War Diary	Cuinchy	12/05/1915	20/05/1915
War Diary	Beuvry	21/05/1915	21/05/1915
War Diary	Annequin	22/05/1915	25/05/1915
War Diary	Tour Biere	26/05/1915	28/05/1915
War Diary	Verqvicneol	29/05/1915	31/05/1915
Heading	3rd Infantry Brigade. 1st Division. War Diary 4th Battn. Royal Welsh Fusiliers June 1915		
War Diary	Verqvigner	01/06/1915	01/06/1915
War Diary	Labeuvriere	02/06/1915	03/06/1915
War Diary	Cuinchy	04/06/1915	10/06/1915
War Diary	Bethune	11/06/1915	24/06/1915
War Diary	Auchel	25/06/1915	28/06/1915
War Diary	Noyelles Les Vermelles	29/06/1915	30/06/1915
Heading	3rd Infantry Brigade. 1st Division. 4th Battn. Royal Welsh Fusiliers July 1915		
War Diary	Noyelles Les Vermelles	01/07/1915	01/07/1915
War Diary	Vermelles	02/07/1915	05/07/1915
War Diary	Fouquereuil	06/07/1915	13/07/1915
War Diary	Cuinchy	14/07/1915	19/07/1915
War Diary	Cambrin	20/08/1915	25/08/1915
War Diary	Verquin	26/08/1915	31/08/1915
Heading	3rd Infantry Brigade. 1st Division. (Became Pioneers to 47th Division 1.9.15.) War Diary 4th Battn. Royal Welsh Fusiliers August 1915		
War Diary	Noyelles-Les-Vermelles	01/08/1915	05/08/1915
War Diary	Vermelles	06/08/1915	12/08/1915
War Diary	Brett River Camp	13/08/1915	18/08/1915
War Diary	Annequin	19/08/1915	22/08/1915
War Diary	Cambrin	22/08/1915	27/08/1915
War Diary	Maison Rouge Cambrin	28/08/1915	31/08/1915

WO 95
1280/2

4 Bttn Royal Welsh Fusiliers

1 Div
3 Infantry Brig

1ST DIVISION
3RD INFANTRY BRIGADE

4TH BATTALION

ROYAL WELCH FUSILIERS

1914 NOV - ~~DEC 1914~~ 1915 AUG

To 47 DIV (PIONEERS)

1ST DIVISION
3RD BRIGADE

4TH BATTALION
ROYAL WELCH FUSILIERS
JAN - AUG 1915

File with 3rd Brigade.

1st Division.

Battalion disembarked Havre 6.11.14.

Joined 3rd Brigade 6th December 1914.

4th BATTALION

ROYAL WELCH FUSILIERS.

NOVEMBER 1 9 1 4

WAR DIARY
or
INTELLIGENCE SUMMARY.
(Erase heading not required.)

Army Form C. 2118.

Instructions regarding War Diaries and Intelligence Summaries are contained in F.S. Regs., Part II. and the Staff Manual respectively. Title pages will be prepared in manuscript.

Hour, Date, Place		Summary of Events and Information	Remarks and references to Appendices
10.10 a.m. 5th Nov. Northampton.		Half Battn. (A.B.C & D. Coys.) Left Northampton. Arrived Southampton 5 p.m.	1/2/3
1 p.m. 5th Nov. "		Half Battn. (E.F.G. & H. Coys.) Left Northampton. Arrived Southampton 8 p.m.	
9 " 5th Nov. Southampton		Embarked whole Battn. on Admiralty Transport Architect. Sailed at 11.30 p.m.	
11 a.m. 6th Nov. Le Havre		Calm voyage and arrived outside Le Havre 11 a.m. The 6th Nov. Lay outside the Harbour with other Transports until 5 p.m. when we entered the Harbour and made fast alongside at 8 p.m. Battalion disembarked and marched off, led by Guide, to rest Camp at Bleville, about 3 miles on high ground above Havre. Arrived at the rest camp, in dense fog, about 2 a.m. on the 7th Nov? and	
2 a.m. 7th Nov. Bleville Camp.		occupied tents. easy picketed.	
10 a.m. 7th Nov. Bleville		Kit inspection.	
2 p.m. " " "		Inspection of Battalion by Camp Commandant. Weather foggy. The 13th Battn. having been acting outpost at Northampton, at Northampton on the 4th Nov?	
10 a.m. 8th Nov "		Rifle inspection and equipment cleaned up camp and after	
3 p.m. 8th Nov "		dinner at 3 p.m. marched out of camp to station at Havre. Experienced a long wait until 8.30 p.m. when the whole	
8.30 p.m. 8th Nov. Havre.		Battalion entrained and left Havre.	

Army Form C. 2118.

WAR DIARY
or
INTELLIGENCE SUMMARY.
(Erase heading not required.)

Instructions regarding War Diaries and Intelligence Summaries are contained in F.S. Regs., Part II. and the Staff Manual respectively. Title pages will be prepared in manuscript.

Hour, Date, Place	Summary of Events and Information	Remarks and references to Appendices
9th Nov. Journey to Saint Omer	Travelled by train via Abbeville, and after short stay there left for St. Omer at 11.30 a.m. Arrived at St. Omer at 7.30 p.m. Detrained and marched into Cavalry barracks (old barracks) at 11 p.m. where quarters were taken for the night.	
10th Nov. St. Omer. 9-30 a.m.	Marched out of Cavalry barracks into Infantry barracks at St. Omer and took up quarters there at 11.0 a.m. And out "tion ration.	
2.30 p.m. 10th Nov. St Omer	Battalion went on short route march returned to Barracks at 5 p.m. Weather very wet.	
6-30 a.m. 11th Nov. St Omer	Battalion prepared to march out to Henringhem about 5 miles and after breakfast marched out at 8.15 a.m. and arrived at Henringhem at 10 a.m. where the Battalion was billeted	
10 a.m. 11th Nov. Henringhem		
2-15 p.m. 11th Nov. Henringhem	Battalion was paraded at 2-15 p.m. after billeting arrangements completed and was exercised in arm drill and musketry until 4-30 p.m. Weather very wet.	

Army Form C. 2118.

WAR DIARY
or
INTELLIGENCE SUMMARY.
(Erase heading not required.)

Instructions regarding War Diaries and Intelligence Summaries are contained in F. S. Regs., Part II. and the Staff Manual respectively. Title pages will be prepared in manuscript.

Hour, Date, Place	Summary of Events and Information	Remarks and references to Appendices
9-30 a.m. 12th Nov. Neuvinghem	Battalion paraded and was inspected by the General Churchester ∧ also being steviced in Musketry. ∧ Reserve troops (passed in the General summary)	
2.15 p.m. 12th Nov. Neuvinghem	Battalion exercised in the attack on ground about 1½ miles from Neuvinghem, adopting the double company and platoon formation for the first time.	
6-30 p.m. 12th Nov. Neuvinghem	Lecture to officers by Col. Frances Hayhurst on the attack with observations on the day's work.	
8-15 p.m. 12th Nov. Neuvinghem	Lecture by O.C. to N.C.O's of Battalion on the attack and observations deduced from the day's work. Received first Tobacco ration. Heard the guns on the Battle line.	

WAR DIARY
or
INTELLIGENCE SUMMARY.
(Erase heading not required.)

Army Form C. 2118.

Hour, Date, Place	Summary of Events and Information	Remarks and references to Appendices
8. a.m. 13th Novr. 1914	Battalion parade marched 2½ miles to high ground above St Omer and after instructions by Col. Cowan R.E. (Staff) the Battalion dug trenches. During the digging rain commenced and continued the rest of the day. The Battalion returned about 1.p.m. the weather being exceptionally severe. In the afternoon the C.O. held a round table discussion amongst the O.C. Companies as to methods of commencing to dig trenches ~test~ armed with least delay and invited suggestions. In the evening lectures by C.O. to N.C.O.s During the afternoon rifle inspection by Companies.	
8.30 a.m. 14th Novr. 14	Battalion paraded and practised the attack over ground south of Henningham. The attack was inspected by General Chichester who held a pow wow of officers after the attack.	
1.p.m " "	After dinner the Battalion proceeded on a route march of about 5 miles and practised taking cover from aeroplanes and adopting	

WAR DIARY
or
INTELLIGENCE SUMMARY.
(Erase heading not required.)

Army Form C. 2118.

Instructions regarding War Diaries and Intelligence Summaries are contained in F. S. Regs., Part II. and the Staff Manual respectively. Title pages will be prepared in manuscript.

Hour, Date, Place	Summary of Events and Information	Remarks and references to Appendices
6.p.m 14th Novr.	artillery formations en route. Lecture by C.O to N.C.Os. on attack formations	
9 a.m 15th Novr.	Battalion paraded and went route marching about 7 miles in a heavy rain. During the march the men became very footsore evidence that the boots issued by the Govt. to the men at Northampton the day before the Battalion left there, were of the most inferior quality, and the C.O. gave orders for O.C. Companies to indent for new boots. The Battalion heard with deep regret of the death of Lord Roberts at Ypres.	
8 a.m 16th Novr.	Battalion paraded and marched to high ground about 1½ miles N. of Henneyham and dug trenches until 4.p.m. Some of the trenches had been partly dug by some other battalion and were partly full of water. The men were instructed in draining	
4.p.m.		
6 p.m. 16th Novr.	the trenches into the traverses. Weather very wet. Lecture to O.C. Companies by C.O.	

WAR DIARY
or
INTELLIGENCE SUMMARY.
(Erase heading not required.)

Army Form C. 2118.

Hour, Date, Place	Summary of Events and Information	Remarks and references to Appendices
8.15 a.m. Nov 17. 1914	Battalion paraded. Half battalion marched to high ground N.W. of Henuytera and was practiced in taking up outpost duties and positions whilst the other half was engaged in firing ball cartridge at targets placed in the fields nearer Henuytera. This was the first opportunity the men had had of firing from the new rifle and despite the heavy showers of rain and sleet made very good practice. Several bullets ricochetted over the hill in front of the firing position and considering the fact that, according to instructions from the General, the ground behind the hill had not been cleared of people, the officers were relieved to hear that no casualties had occurred. During the afternoon the half battalions reversed occupations the first half doing outpost work and the 2nd half firing target practice.	

Army Form C. 2118.

WAR DIARY
or
INTELLIGENCE SUMMARY.
(Erase heading not required.)

Instructions regarding War Diaries and Intelligence Summaries are contained in F.S. Regs., Part II. and the Staff Manual respectively. Title pages will be prepared in manuscript.

Hour, Date, Place	Summary of Events and Information	Remarks and references to Appendices
9. a. m Nov. 17. 1914 (Continued)	A detachment of 20 men under Lt. W. Hugh-Jones left by motor Bus for St Omer to represent the Battalion at the funeral of Lord Roberts F.M. The body was taken to England for burial in St Paul Cathedral.	
8.30 am Nov. 18. 1914	Battalion went for a route march of about 16 miles the day being spent in placing context to previous days. The route was via Thérouanne Nertalle, Relegard & Relyne	
8.30 am Nov. 19. 1914	Battalion paraded and started the right half battalion practice the attack with ball ammunition. The left half Battalion under Major Johnson was instructed in musketry. Snow fell during the afternoon and the Battalion returned. Rifle + feet inspection during the rest of the day, and lecture by the C.O. to officers on the attack.	

Army Form C. 2118.

WAR DIARY
or
INTELLIGENCE SUMMARY.
(Erase heading not required.)

Instructions regarding War Diaries and Intelligence Summaries are contained in F. S. Regs., Part II. and the Staff Manual respectively. Title pages will be prepared in manuscript.

Hour, Date, Place	Summary of Events and Information	Remarks and references to Appendices
8.30 a.m. Nov 20th 1914	Battalion marched to ground N. of Henningham and engaged in completing and digging Trenches until 4 p.m. Weather very clear and frosty. Snow being about 2" deep. News received that first four since they left Northampton but owing to lack of enterprise on the part of the inhabitants the men were unable to change the notes which had been paid home.	
8.30 a.m. Nov 21st 1914	Battalion proceeded on route march via Belle Croix Ave. Robecq Hezques about 18 miles. Several French detachments were passed en route. The ground was most slippery, the snow having been frozen over, made the march somewhat trying.	
2 p.m. Nov 22nd 1914. Sunday	Battalion practiced in the attack on ground S. of Henningham. The ground was hard & snow covered. About 1 p.m. on the Battalion	

Army Form C. 2118.

WAR DIARY
or
INTELLIGENCE SUMMARY.
(Erase heading not required.)

Instructions regarding War Diaries and Intelligence Summaries are contained in F.S. Regs., Part II. and the Staff Manual respectively. Title pages will be prepared in manuscript.

Hour, Date, Place	Summary of Events and Information	Remarks and references to Appendices
9. a.m. Nov. 23rd.14	Went on route march of about 10 miles via Belle Croix. The men felt the effects of the bad boots, in some cases the soles of the boots leaving the uppers. Under Major Johnson. First half battalion marched to high ground above Pellendifue and practised outpost scheme whilst 2nd half Battalion practised the attack near Esques. In the afternoon the 1st half Battalion practised the attack before General Chichester.	
9.a.m. Nov. 2? 14.	One of the transport horses foaled but both horse & foal died. Capt Shearn R.S.Fus. joined the Battalion as Adjutant. Companies placed at disposal of Company officers during the morning and rifle, feet & billet inspections were held.	
2. p.m. Nov. 23.14.	Battalion went route march via Esque about 7 miles having first been addressed by the Colonel who read General	

WAR DIARY
or
INTELLIGENCE SUMMARY.
(Erase heading not required.)

Army Form C. 2118.

Hour, Date, Place	Summary of Events and Information	Remarks and references to Appendices
	order by F.M. Sir John French to the troops under his command appreciative of work done and giving general summary & survey of the war and situation. In his address to the Battalion the Colonel expressed the thanks of himself & the Battalion to Lt. Soroney Suffolk who had succeeded Capt Ford as adjutant and who now resigned his position in favour of Capt. Rees.	
9 a.m. Nov. 25th. 14	Batt. paraded. A B. C & D Coys under Major Johnson proceeded to ground E of Bhaudecque and took up position [practice]. The attack until 1 p.m. E F G & H. Coys practiced in Musketry - firing ball ammunition into wood N E of Esques.	
2.p.m. Nov. 25th. 14	A B. C & D Coys engaged in Musketry E F G & H. " under Major Nelson practised the attack.	

Army Form C. 2118.

WAR DIARY
or
INTELLIGENCE SUMMARY.
(Erase heading not required.)

Instructions regarding War Diaries and Intelligence Summaries are contained in F.S. Regs., Part II. and the Staff Manual respectively. Title pages will be prepared in manuscript.

Hour, Date, Place	Summary of Events and Information	Remarks and references to Appendices
7-45 Nov. 26th/14 Henninghen	Battalion paraded and marched to Wadresque Dug trenches along the bank of the canal. This being the same canal as at Ypres. Bath returned 5.30 p.m. The C.O. & Adjutant lectured to Officers after mess.	
9.a.m 27th Nov. Henninghen	Companies paraded under Company officers & were engaged in inspections when General Chetode arrived and ordered an attack. This was carried out near the village of Helfant. The General being expressed his satisfaction with the attack. The Battalion marched home via Helfant & Blanderque about 7-8 miles. Weather very wet	
9.a.m Nov. 28. Henninghen	Battn paraded and marched along Rouen road about 8 miles and after dinners practised a vanguard action from Helfant to Bilcque. B C D E & F Coys under Major	

Army Form C. 2118.

WAR DIARY
or
INTELLIGENCE SUMMARY.
(Erase heading not required.)

Instructions regarding War Diaries and Intelligence Summaries are contained in F.S. Regs., Part II. and the Staff Manual respectively. Title pages will be prepared in manuscript.

Hour, Date, Place	Summary of Events and Information	Remarks and references to Appendices
Nov 29. 9 a.m. Kennyhun Sunday.	Wilson represented a retiring force and A Coy. by 2 under Major Johnson the pursuing force. The action developed into an interesting situation when dartness stopped the pursuit & the Battalion returned home to billets the C.O. having previously announced his success in obtaining a day of rest & for the Battn the following day. Voluntary Church Parade followed by Holy Communion in the Schoolroom. This was the first day of rest the Battn had experienced since landing and was much appreciated the men took the much desired opportunity to wash clothes & no duty or parades lasting until dark, left little time for personal attention. The service was taken by Chaplain Major	

Army Form C. 2118.

WAR DIARY
or
INTELLIGENCE SUMMARY.
(Erase heading not required.)

Instructions regarding War Diaries and Intelligence Summaries are contained in F. S. Regs., Part II. and the Staff Manual respectively. Title pages will be prepared in manuscript.

Hour, Date, Place	Summary of Events and Information	Remarks and references to Appendices
9 a.m Nov 30th Herringhen	Battalion marched through Herssonne about 7 miles and after divine again practised the war game action of the previous Saturday. The same coy. took up the various positions. The day again proved most interesting and instructive if somewhat fatiguing for owing to heavy rain the fields being all plough[ed] & arable proved heavy going and the action took place over 3 miles of country	
9 a.m Dec 1st Herringhen	Marched to ground N. of Herssonne & practised on 1/2 mile the attack up to 200 yards of the position when the Battalion was ordered to dig itself in. Two hours were given for this purpose & proved sufficient. The supply of ammunition was brought up by the mules [for this purpose proved satisfactory]	

3rd Brigade.
1st Division.

Battalion joined 3rd Brigade
from L of C. 8th December'14.

4th BATTALION

ROYAL WELCH FUSILIERS

DECEMBER 1914

WAR DIARY

Copied from last page of War Diary for November

9 a.m. Dec. 1st	Marched to ground N. of THEROUANNE and practised the attack over 1½ miles up to 200 yards of the position when the battalion was ordered to dig itself in.
HERNINGHEM.	Two hours were given for this purpose and proved sufficient. The supply of ammunition was brought up by the mules and properly distributed.

WAR DIARY or INTELLIGENCE SUMMARY.

Army Form C. 2118.

(Erase heading not required.)

Hour, Date, Place	Summary of Events and Information	Remarks and references to Appendices
2nd Decr. 9 a.m. Hennuyken	Battalion paraded and marched to scene of yesterdays practice. The attack was again carried out took place before Genl. Chichester. The objective had been altered to hay loft and provided an interesting lesson. The Battalion entrenched itself in the afternoon. Before leaving for billets the Colonel announced to the Battn. that we were under orders to move & that we were attached to the 3rd Brigade of the 1st Army.	
3rd Decr. 9 a.m. Hennuyken to Vaudricque	Battalion marched to Vaudricque & completed the trenches begun along the bank of the canal. Most of the marching was done in very heavy rain & hail	

WAR DIARY
or
INTELLIGENCE SUMMARY.
(Erase heading not required.)

Army Form C. 2118.

Hour, Date, Place	Summary of Events and Information	Remarks and references to Appendices
4th Decr 1914 9 a.m. Henninghem	Battalion took up an outpost position 1 mile in & led on ground S. of Bleuecque & after dinner went route marching. All the officers were granted leave to go to St Omer to purchase British warms &c during the afternoon	
5th Decr 1914 9 a.m. Henninghem	Stormy day. Hail & snow. Companies paraded under Company Officers & inspection held. All the billets were inspected and stated 5 men's deficiencies made good. During the day a French Cavalry Division passed through the village. A day of packing up preparatory to moving	
6th Decr 1914 Henninghem to Hazebrouck	Breakfast 6 a.m. Battalion moved out of Henninghem at 9 a.m. and marched via Wardrecques to Hazebrouck. Arriving there at 2-30 p.m. The distance being 13-14 miles	

WAR DIARY
or
INTELLIGENCE SUMMARY.
(Erase heading not required.)

Army Form C. 2118.

Hour, Date, Place	Summary of Events and Information	Remarks and references to Appendices
7th Dec. 1912 Hazebrouck to Bailleul	The last 6 miles of the march was over "pave" & found fatiguing. Our advance party under Major Wilson arrived in Hazebrouck in time to see a German aeroplane fly over the Town. It dropped two bombs which killed 9 men of the Lancs Regt. & a few civilians. The Battalion billeted the night. Here I heard details of the meeting in the town a few days previously of H. M. the King, the President of the French Republic, King Albert, Genl French & Genl Joffre. Battalion marched to Bailleul. Most of the road being "pave". The distance about 9 miles. Arrived at Bailleul about 2 p.m. & the battalion billeted. The march was frequently delayed by supply trains passing on the narrow road.	

Army Form C. 2118.

WAR DIARY
or
INTELLIGENCE SUMMARY.
(Erase heading not required.)

Instructions regarding War Diaries and Intelligence Summaries are contained in F.S. Regs., Part II. and the Staff Manual respectively. Title pages will be prepared in manuscript.

Hour, Date, Place	Summary of Events and Information	Remarks and references to Appendices
Dec 8th 15/14 Bailleul 10 a.m. – 2.15 p.m.	Battalion paraded & was inspected by Companies & by Sir David Henderson the Commander of the Burrows. Battalion paraded & marched to ground N.W. of town about 1½ miles out and addressed by the C.O. on importance of taking care of arms &c. Returned at 4 p.m.	
5.15 p.m.	Battalion paraded & marched to same ground & by Companies dug trenches until 11.30 p.m. Water flowing into some trenches somewhat retarded work	
9 Dec 1914 Bailleul 10 a.m.	Companies paraded under Company officers & inspected. Boots proved to be greatly needed. The supply being insufficient for needs	
2 p.m. – 6 p.m.	Battalion route marched 8 miles via heavies	

WAR DIARY
or
INTELLIGENCE SUMMARY.

(Erase heading not required.)

Army Form C. 2118.

Hour, Date, Place	Summary of Events and Information	Remarks and references to Appendices
10th Dec. 1914 Bailleul	The Battalion was at home as the Brigade was Brigade in waiting so the opportunity was taken to supply & fit out men with deficiencies.	
2 p.m.	Battalion taken to the trenches dug on the night of the 8th & the faults observed. During the day comforts sent by friends in Wrexham were distributed to the men.	
11th Dec. 1914	Battalion stood to arms	
6.15 a.m. - 8.30		
9 - 12 a.m.	Battalion practised by Companies relieving in the trenches dug on the night of the 8th inst.	
12 - 1 p.m.	Lecture by C.O. to Officers	
2 p.m. to 5	Battalion marched to an allotted N of Bailleul-Nieuhtein Road and practised attack by double Companies before General Butler. the Brigadier who advised the men	

WAR DIARY or INTELLIGENCE SUMMARY.

(Erase heading not required.)

Army Form C. 2118.

Instructions regarding War Diaries and Intelligence Summaries are contained in F.S. Regs., Part II. and the Staff Manual respectively. Title pages will be prepared in manuscript.

Hour, Date, Place	Summary of Events and Information	Remarks and references to Appendices
Bailleul 12th Decr. 9.15	Companies paraded under Company officers until 12.15. Lectures & instruction in bayonet attacks & bayonet drill	
1 p.m – 5 p.m	Coy Battalion marched to allotted area near Railway & practised Battalion attack occupying artillery position first & advancing from firing line when unit up by Signal advances. General Butler to visited the Battalion during the practise	
10 a.m & 3 p.m 13th Decr. Bailleul	Church parades in billets occupied by 1st Half Battalion	
5 a.m 14th Decr. Bailleul	Rained all 5 a.m and battalion ordered to be in readiness to move by 7 a.m afterwards from 7 a.m battalion ordered to stand by & Companies were paraded with their Officers from	

Forms/C. 2118/10

Army Form C. 2118.

WAR DIARY
or
INTELLIGENCE SUMMARY.
(Erase heading not required.)

Instructions regarding War Diaries and Intelligence Summaries are contained in F. S. Regs., Part II. and the Staff Manual respectively. Title pages will be prepared in manuscript.

Hour, Date, Place	Summary of Events and Information	Remarks and references to Appendices
3 – 5 p.m. 14th Decr. Bailleul	3 p.m – 5 p.m exchanging & falling boots. Capt J. B. Perry invalided to hospital with Rheumatism	
9 – 30 a.m. 15th Decr. Bailleul	Battalion under orders to stand by ready to move at 2 hours notice. Paraded by half Battalions under Censor and Junior Major and inspected as to making of tents, waterproof sheets, trimmers. Lieut Bouffignac attached to regiment for 3 days promotion on leave thereof. Lieut C. L. Davies invalided to hospital	
16th Decr. 9 a.m. Bailleul	Brigade trip in washing. Companies were paraded and in Company officers at 11 a.m. Lectures & inspections Lecture by Adjutant & Platoon Commanders	

Army Form C. 2118.

WAR DIARY
or
INTELLIGENCE SUMMARY.
(Erase heading not required.)

Instructions regarding War Diaries and Intelligence Summaries are contained in F.S. Regs., Part II. and the Staff Manual respectively. Title pages will be prepared in manuscript.

Hour, Date, Place	Summary of Events and Information	Remarks and references to Appendices
16th Sept. 1914 Bailleul 3 p.m.	Paraded by half battalions and under Major Johnson and Major Latham and inspected by them	
9.30 a.m. 17th Sept (Bailleul)	Route march in vicinity of billets and lectures on shooting aeroplanes	
2-15 p.m.	Battalion paraded under Company arrangements (musketry)	
– 4-30 pm	in aeroplane shooting and physical drill	
18th Sept 9 a.m.	Battalion ordered to be in readiness to move at 2 hours notice paraded at 9 a m and the aeroplane arrived over us in Platoon drill	
2 – 5 p.m.	Company parades	

Army Form C. 2118.

WAR DIARY
or
INTELLIGENCE SUMMARY.
(Erase heading not required.)

Instructions regarding War Diaries and Intelligence Summaries are contained in F.S. Regs., Part II. and the Staff Manual respectively. Title pages will be prepared in manuscript.

Hour, Date, Place	Summary of Events and Information	Remarks and references to Appendices
10 a.m. 19th Dec.? Bailleul 10ᵃᵐ – 12-30 p.m.	Battalion parade the order to be in readiness to move at 24 hours notice withdrawn. Companies practised in Platoon drill. Surg. Capt Anderson reported a case of scarlet fever in the billets occupied by A B & D Companies and steps were instantly taken to isolate these Companies in their billets	
1-15 p.m – 5 p–	C, B, & H.Q. Companies marched to allotted areas & practised the attack. General Bulfin visited the Battalion during the practise	
20th Decr. 1914 3 p.m	Voluntary Church parade for men of 1st & 3rd Coys in those officers mess	
5. p.m	Battalion moved to more immediately with the remainder of the Brigade.	

WAR DIARY
or
INTELLIGENCE SUMMARY.
(Erase heading not required.)

Army Form C. 2118.

Instructions regarding War Diaries and Intelligence Summaries are contained in F.S. Regs., Part II. and the Staff Manual respectively. Title pages will be prepared in manuscript.

Hour, Date, Place	Summary of Events and Information	Remarks and references to Appendices
7 p.m. 20th Sept. Bailleul	Battalion left Bailleul & marched [in rear of Brigade] to Hinville which was reached [by the Battalion] at 1-30 a.m. on the 21st [civilians about]	
1-30 a.m. 21st Sept. Hinville to Béthune	Battalion rested in billets until 4 a.m. & marched out of Hinville [with Brigade (Munster Battalion in rear of Battalion)] to Béthune arriving outside Béthune 7-30 a.m. – 8 a.m. where the Brigade halted. [Railway officers were called for and Battalion under the impression that billets were to be occupied did not cook any meals. Arrived outside 12-30 was wet, cold & bleak weather, very much wanting hot food especially as no other battalions had Travelling Cookers & were supplying men with hot drinks & food.] Brigade halted	
12-30 p.m.	C.O. and adjutant called to head of Brigade and then ordered to march to attack enemy at Hazebrouck some 7-8 miles distant. The Gloucester and South Wales	

Army Form C. 2118.

WAR DIARY
or
INTELLIGENCE SUMMARY.
(Erase heading not required.)

Instructions regarding War Diaries and Intelligence Summaries are contained in F. S. Regs., Part II. and the Staff Manual respectively. Title pages will be prepared in manuscript.

Hour, Date, Place	Summary of Events and Information	Remarks and references to Appendices
23rd Dec/1914 Festubert	Borderers led the attack which commenced at 2-15 p.m. with the 2nd Welch Regt in Support and the Munsters and 4th R Welsh Fusiliers in Reserve. Arriving at Leave the Brigade came under artillery fire. Our battalion marched on the right of our guns + for the first time as a Battalion came under fire, the enemys guns shelling our guns which were 50 - 100 yards on our left the attack continued until driven on the 22nd had our Battalion being on the left of the attack was not called into the front line but took cover behind a ruined building _____ some 800 yards from the enemys front resting orders a few moments. The enemy had ranged during the advance. the Brigade casualties had proved during the advance, the Brigade suffered heavy losses. About 7 a.m. rations arrived and we had our first real meal since leaving the 20th having marched about 25 miles. After breakfast the Battalion marched	

Forms/C. 2118/10

Army Form C. 2118.

WAR DIARY
or
INTELLIGENCE SUMMARY.
(Erase heading not required.)

Hour, Date, Place	Summary of Events and Information	Remarks and references to Appendices

23rd Dec: 1914
Festubert
5. p.m

to a small plantation in rear of the village of Festubert and about 2 p.m was ordered to fill up a gap in the firing line. Subsequently the order was altered and the Battalion took possession of some dug outs on the Rue Festubert end of Festubert at about 7. a.m. No: 1 & 4 Companies were opened to man the reserve trenches and at 2 a.m the remainder of the Battalion moved to billets vacated by the Highland Light Infantry. Brown's traverse. Major Johnson received a Severe contusion) Lieut. & 4 Companies in the trenches. Capt Davies and Capt Wilkie wounded & sent to hospital

24th Dec: 1914

A frosty night succeeded the previous wet weather and caused many men to be numbers with cold feet

Forms/C. 2118/10

Army Form C. 2118.

1/2 3

WAR DIARY
or
INTELLIGENCE SUMMARY.
(Erase heading not required.)

Hour, Date, Place	Summary of Events and Information	Remarks and references to Appendices
24th Decr 1914 5 p.m	Pte E Hughes 8 Coy was killed and Cpl [E Jones] wounded in the Trenches. The firing had been heavy. Coys 1 + 4 Coys relieved Nos 2 + 3 in the Trenches	
25th Decr 1914 5.30 a.m	Nos 2 + 3 Coy relieved Nos 1 + 4 in the Trenches. The day was fine and up to 6.12 noon perfectly quiet. During the afternoon the village of Tabuteten was shelled + a few dropped near the Trenches. At 8 p.m a report was received of a German movement on our front – the Battalion stood ready for the attack	
26th Decr 1914 5.30 a.m	Nos 1 + 4 Coys relieved Nos 2 + 3 in the Trenches + work of improving the trenches proceeded. Heavy artillery shells in the afternoon at 12.15 a.m	
27th Decr 1914 12.15 a.m	Report received by Brigade from observer of expected German attack and the Battalion stood to arms	

Army Form C. 2118.

WAR DIARY
or
INTELLIGENCE SUMMARY.
(Erase heading not required.)

Instructions regarding War Diaries and Intelligence Summaries are contained in F.S. Regs., Part II. and the Staff Manual respectively. Title pages will be prepared in manuscript.

Hour, Date, Place	Summary of Events and Information	Remarks and references to Appendices
27th Decr 1914 cont	The Enemy shelled our position during the afternoon and wounded 3 men of C Coy. [Pte Pelming J B Coy was shot in the head in the Trenches reinforcements]	1/2/3
27th Decr 1914 Zealebeck 5.30 a.m.	The day was very wet and the Trenches soon began to fill with water which caused the Coys in the Trenches some trouble in repairing & improving the same. No 2 & 3 Coys relieved No 1 & 4 in the Trenches	
28th Decr 1914 Zealebeck	Xmas parcels arrived containing many comforts. No 1 & 4 Coys relieved No 2 & 3 Coys in the Trenches. The weather & wet Trenches caused many cases of Rheumatism and sore feet. The Village was shelled during the afternoon. Lt. C.L. Berry evacuated to hospital at Bernes Three other men in the hospital on account of sickness.	
29th Decr 1914 5.30 a.m.	Heavy thunderstorm during the morning added. No 2 & 3 Coys relieved No 1 & 4 Coys, the Trenches were very wet & necessitated much repair. Lt. Harvey	

Army Form C. 2118.

WAR DIARY
or
INTELLIGENCE SUMMARY.
(Erase heading not required.)

Instructions regarding War Diaries and Intelligence Summaries are contained in F.S. Regs., Part II. and the Staff Manual respectively. Title pages will be prepared in manuscript.

Hour, Date, Place	Summary of Events and Information	Remarks and references to Appendices
29th Decr 1914 6 p.m.	Watts has been at Isthuueaire the 21st inst with his platoon as baggage guard arrived in Furnes.	1/2³
30th Decr 1914 5.30 a.m.	Very bright moonlight night observed enemy aeroplane very busy. Nos 2 + 3 Coys relieved by Nos 1 + 4 Coys in the trenches. The usual shelling by the enemy occurred during the afternoon. [German aeroplane's bombs aimed at position.]	
3rd Decr 1914 5-30 a.m.	Nos 1 + 4 Coys relieved by Nos 2 + 8 Coys. Trenches repaired. Report received by Brigade of enemy movement. Caused Battalion to stand to arms for 2 hours at night. Usual artillery duel during afternoon.	
3 p.m.	Rifle inspection by C.O.	
1st Jany 1915 5-30 a.m.	Nos 2 + 3 Coys relieved by Nos 1 + 4 Coys. By orders of the Brigadier the outgoing Coys were	

1st Division
3rd Brigade.

W A R   D I A R Y

4th ROYAL WELCH FUSILIERS

January

1 9 1 5

WAR DIARY

Copied from the last page of the War Diary for December 1914.

1st January 1915   Nos. 2 & 3 Coys. reliebed by Nos. 1 & 4 Coys.
5.30 a.m.
                   By orders of the Brigadier the inlying Coys. were -

                                                        Continued on next page.

Army Form C. 2118

WAR DIARY
or
INTELLIGENCE SUMMARY.
(Erase heading not required.)

Instructions regarding War Diaries and Intelligence Summaries are contained in F. S. Regs., Part II. and the Staff Manual respectively. Title pages will be prepared in manuscript.

Hour, Date, Place	Summary of Events and Information	Remarks and references to Appendices
2 Jan 1915 3 p.m.	engaged in loopholing walls of village & putting village in state of proper defence	1/23
5-30 a.m. Festubert	Rifles inspected by C.O. Lt Harrup invalided [to hospital]	
3rd Jany 1915 3 p.m. Festubert	No. 2 & 3 Coys relieved No 1 & 4 Coys in the Trenches. Platoon of No 2 by error of Guide went to party trench of Gloucesters. Village and Trenches shelled by enemy during the day they rest. Rifle Inspection 2 p.m.	
5-30 a.m. 3 p.m.	No. 1 & 4 Coys relieved No. 2 & 3 Coys in the Trenches. During the afternoon the outgoing Coys were employed in cleaning up the village streets. Rifle inspection by C.O.	

WAR DIARY
or
INTELLIGENCE SUMMARY.
(Erase heading not required.)

Army Form C. 2118.

Hour, Date, Place	Summary of Events and Information	Remarks and references to Appendices
3 Jan 15/14 continued	Lieut: Rouppner took platoon of No 4 Coy to Thrower Ridli ferry trench for 24 hours preservation. Lieut Ricardo took platoon of No 4 Coy to Gloucester Regt trench trench for 24 hours for instruction. Lieut Hugh Smith took platoon of No 1 Coy to Welsh Regt trench trench for 24 hours for instruction. Capt Ashdown & No 1 Coy being wounded in the leg whilst going to the trenches.	
4th Jany 1914. 5-30 a.m.	Nos 1 + 3 Coys returned. Nos 1 + 4 Coys in the trenches and men of E Coy being wounded whilst going to the trenches. Lieut Clayton took platoon of E & F Coys Regt trench to Welsh trenches for 24 hours instruction.	
8. p.m.	Rifle inspection by C.O. Lieut O.S. Thomas evacuated [to hospital]	

WAR DIARY
or
INTELLIGENCE SUMMARY.
(Erase heading not required.)

Army Form C. 2118

Hour, Date, Place	Summary of Events and Information	Remarks and references to Appendices
5th Jany 1915 5-30 a.m trenches.	Nos 1 & 4 Coys relieved Nos 2 & 8 Coys in the trenches 1 Capt [Major A Coy was] shot dead during the morning [Erased] in trenches] Battalion much reduced in fighting strength owing to prevalence of Rheumatism "Trench feet" due to the water in trenches caused them 2 feet deep. R.P. Roberts Capt. & Bath R.W.Fus. — J.C. FauceMayfuik Lt Col Comdg 4th Btn 5th Reg.Fus. Jan 5th 1915.	

WAR DIARY 4th Bn. Roy. Welsh Fus. (T.)
or
INTELLIGENCE SUMMARY.

(Erase heading not required.)

Army Form C. 2118.

Hour, Date, Place	Summary of Events and Information	Remarks and references to Appendices
6 to 8 April 1915 Festubert	No changes in situation. Rifleys carried out. Number of men sent to hospital with trench wounds no very remarkable	
	On 8th about midnight 19th Bengal Lancers relieved the battalion, which marched into Bethune where billets were on arrival	
9 to 14 Bethune	In reserve at Bethune. Visited by Div. Gen. & also the General commanding 2nd Army who expressed his satisfaction at the improvement of the Battn. [The Battn had had an enormous amount of sickness, and had been without a roof known during 19 days, a day not being enjoyed in safety a few days rest was important, no casualties]	A/2-3
2.45 pm 14 Jan Bethune	Regd orders to return to trenches at Givenchy. Billeted at Beuvry, north of Bethune for remainder of night. So very many of the week Ryf. death in the Bethune mining district.	
15 am Givenchy	The above companies remained in trenches during 48 hours and of 24 as forewarned. The organ of trench is to be rather an long way apart & no time was always sure. The changes of casualties above referred to were due to no longer use hopeful warm weather habitually carefully carried through, but a little more inclemently. Everything went satisfactorily.	

Army Form C. 2118.

WAR DIARY
or
INTELLIGENCE SUMMARY.
(Erase heading not required.)

Instructions regarding War Diaries and Intelligence Summaries are contained in F.S. Regs., Part II. and the Staff Manual respectively. Title pages will be prepared in manuscript.

Hour, Date, Place	Summary of Events and Information	Remarks and references to Appendices
15 – 24 Jan 1915 Givenchy	Patrols a nuit and normally. Men other in trenches engaged in improving them. No fire broken supplies to all who come in. But for mishap and hardly any casualties. Enemy shelling village occasionally alternated machine gun posture.	
Jan 25 "	Heavy bombardment of Givenchy village and trenches continued for 2 hours. In all our troops also came under [Pte "Metal" Trench was somewhat but immediately recommenced towards a communication trench. Damage to trenches took all the enemy with [*illegible*] During the action the 4th R.W. & 2 companies of the [*illegible*] Scotts. P Grand. At Maylesterne and 50 m. 10 toss. high & 4/5 were at some small outposts on the trench but failed to reach it. Enemy made some attempts to bring forward and on more tops about 10 Yds. or more of French being held by [*illegible*] 62 & 6 x 1 m b of about [*illegible*] this depth. One company was sent to support to support mostly of what this extremely must up and hard beaten the enemy retired (under [*illegible*]) and was sent enforced to scored ground. One cov. of 2 regiment Rusens Grenadiers Rose but an [*illegible*] Rifleman 50 men left part of Brigade were petitioned by the G.R. Reserve and later commander. Troops all the the R.R. Reserve and the engineers were also needed the engineers [*illegible*] & Brigade	0/2 3

Army Form C. 2118.

WAR DIARY
or
INTELLIGENCE SUMMARY.
(Erase heading not required.)

Instructions regarding War Diaries and Intelligence Summaries are contained in F.S. Regs., Part II. and the Staff Manual respectively. Title pages will be prepared in manuscript.

Hour, Date, Place	Summary of Events and Information	Remarks and references to Appendices
26 – 31/Jan/1915 Gueudy	Relief as usual. Enemy's further shelling and enemy defences. Daily shelling and sniping by our & enemy's artillery.	

J. Hw Hunt Lt. Col.
Comdg. 4th Bn. Roy. Sussex Regt.

1=2=15

1st Division
3rd Brigade.

WAR DIARY

4th ROYAL WELCH FUSILIERS

February

1 9 1 5

WAR DIARY
or
INTELLIGENCE SUMMARY. 4 Royal Welsh Fus.
(Erase heading not required.)

Army Form C. 2118.

Instructions regarding War Diaries and Intelligence Summaries are contained in F.S. Regs., Part II. and the Staff Manual respectively. Title pages will be prepared in manuscript.

Hour, Date, Place	Summary of Events and Information	Remarks and references to Appendices
1–3 July 1915 Givenchy	Relief as usual. Working parties, repairs and improving defences.	
6 p.m. 3/7/15	Bn relieved and battalion marched to Marles-les-Mines into huts. Lt Col Evans & Lt Col Davies 2 Lieut J R Williams & W Evans joined.	
4–22 July 1915 Marles-les-Mines	Battalion carried on everyday training, musketry, attack etc. Specialists in machine gun sections, signallers, scouts, report training, employed. Officers, N.C.O's, and men received instruction in several subjects. N.C.O's. received instructions in Bomb Throwing and many were passed trained in bomb throwing. Remainder Bn'n a.c. Rougere. Capt W.R. Elwyn Lt. 2nd Lts R Richards & G G Jones [?] 2nd Lt Parry[?] Battn'n two field officers held a week's leave in England, also several N.C.O's. Battn inspected by G.O.C. 1 Corps.	A/c 3
23 July 1915	Battn marched to ESSARS to billets	
9.0 a.m. 25 July 1915		
26–28 July 1915 Essars	Battalion carried on company training etc.	

1st Division
3rd Brigade.

WAR DIARY

4th ROYAL WELCH FUSILIERS

March

1915

WAR DIARY
or
INTELLIGENCE SUMMARY.
(Erase heading not required.)

Army Form C. 2118.

Hour, Date, Place	Summary of Events and Information	Remarks and references to Appendices
1st March. Essars.	St. David's Day, all ranks wore leeks in their caps. The officers dined together, after being sealed, a white goat (borrowed) with gilded Horns, was led around the table to roll of drums. Drum escorted by a Sergeant Drummer with 2 sticks, effort good. A.mm Officers got a leek each.	
2nd March. Essars.	Bath. occurred in Company training. Worthy parties supplied for divisions work under R.E.	
5, 6th March		
6pm 7th Festubert	Relieved Gloucester Regt. in Section C1 Left half. Quiet day in trenches. Breast works reported not to parapet anywhere. Enemy companions their wire at night.	
8"	Co. operate with General advance by rapid burst of fire at various intervals. Lieut Wood R.E. and 6 men wounded.	
9"		
10"	Quiet day in trenches. Working parties at night filling up gap between Cuinchy and Mamontin. 2 men killed.	
11, 12, 13"		
14"	Patrols sent out to reconnoitre ground at night. Report ground very boggy. Relieved by 1st Bn. Northampton Regt and went to Billets at Long Cornet.	A/2/3
15 – 24"	Bn. was at rest in Billets. Coy. training etc were carried out. In afternoon 24" marched to Neuve Chapelle and relieved Rifle Brigade who were in reserve trenches. Portion were	

Army Form C. 2118

WAR DIARY
or
INTELLIGENCE SUMMARY.
(Erase heading not required.)

Instructions regarding War Diaries and Intelligence Summaries are contained in F. S. Regs., Part II. and the Staff Manual respectively. Title pages will be prepared in manuscript.

Hour, Date, Place	Summary of Events and Information	Remarks and references to Appendices
25th, 27th	Shelled coming up. no casualties. Bn was in reserve Dugouts [Bowers] occupied by Gurmans] Casualties this period 2 men killed an 3 men wounded	
27 – 31st	Bn relieved Glosters Regt in front trenches. casualties 2 men killed and 4 men wounded. Shelling was a daily occurrence. Major Wilson and Capt Y. D. Bury went to hospital on 30th. Bn was relieved on 31st by MUNSTERS and returned to Reserve Dug outs previously occupied by us.	

J.C. James Mayhurst Lieut Col
Comy 4th R.W.F.

Forms/C. 2118/10

3rd Infantry Brigade.
1st Division.

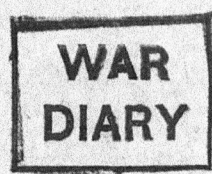

4th BATTN. ROYAL WELCH FUSILIERS.

A P R I L

1 9 1 5

WAR DIARY
or
INTELLIGENCE SUMMARY.
(Erase heading not required.)

Army Form C. 2118.

Place	Date	Hour	Summary of Events and Information	Remarks and references to Appendices
NEUVE CHAPELLE	1.4.15		Bismarck's birthday, nothing unusual occurred, being a fine day men took opportunity of washing. The Gs [being in Reserve] shelling in afternoon, no damage. Casualties 1 man wounded.	
"	2.4.15		Quiet day. Some shelling, 3 men hurt, working party at night. Casualties 1 killed 4 wounded.	
"	3.4.15		Demonstration at 4.30 a.m. in conjunction with operations on R. & L. Quiet day, 400 men London Territorials Bn were sent at 2 P.M. to be shown how to make breastworks & dig communication trench, working party at night. Casualties 1 killed.	W.p 1st - 7th K.2 & 8
"	4.4.15		Relieved West Regt in front line. Draft 41 men arrived. Casualties 2nd Lt in hospital, C.S.M Jones & 1 man wounded.	
"	5.4.15		Quiet day, but very wet. Casualties 2nd Lt H. Owen to hospital & 1 man wounded.	
"	6.4.15		Quiet day, slight shelling H.Q. 5th Sussex Regt. went round trenches, wet in evening. Casualties NIL.	
"	7.4.15		Quiet day, were relieved very late (10 P.M) by 5th Sussex Regt & returned to Le Cheques to Billets. Coys arrived between 1 a.m. & 3 a.m. 6th very tired. No casualties.	

WAR DIARY
or
INTELLIGENCE SUMMARY.
(Erase heading not required.)

Army Form C. 2118.

Instructions regarding War Diaries and Intelligence Summaries are contained in F. S. Regs., Part II. and the Staff Manual respectively. Title pages will be prepared in manuscript.

Place	Date	Hour	Summary of Events and Information	Remarks and references to Appendices
LES CHOCQUES	8-4-15		Bn relied & men had baths by Coy arrangements.	
"	9-4-15		Rested.	
"	10-4-15			
"	11-4-15		Lesson with cookers. Lieut Darlington returned from R.E.	
"	12-4-15		Usual training. Bn exercises in Bois de Pacault, cookers issued to Coys.	
"	13-4-15		Usual training.	
"	14-4-15		Usual training. Adjt & Coy Commdrs went to see the breastworks the Bn is to occupy. Lt Ions got a bullet through his cap.	
RUE-de-L'EPINETTE	15-4-15		Relieved the Black Watch in Sec. D1a. Quiet night.	
"	16-4-15		Quiet day.	
"	17-4-15		Quiet day.	
"	18-4-15		Quiet day.	
"	19-4-15		Coy 23rd London Regt went away & were relieved by C. & D. Coy in Indian Village. 21st London Regt relieved A & B. Coy from front line. A & B Coys on relief went on working party about 10 p.m. casualties. 1 man wounded.	
"	20-4-15		Quiet day.	

Army Form C. 2118.

WAR DIARY
or
INTELLIGENCE SUMMARY.
(Erase heading not required.)

Instructions regarding War Diaries and Intelligence Summaries are contained in F.S. Regs. Part II and the Staff Manual respectively. Title pages will be prepared in manuscript.

Place	Date	Hour	Summary of Events and Information	Remarks and references to Appendices
"	21-4-15		Quiet day, slight shelling. [Working party 2 Officers 180 men at 9.p.m.] Capt. Clough to hospital.	
"	22-4-15		Quiet day, inoperative shelling. [Working party 200 men 9.p.m.]	
"	23-4-15		C & D Coys relieved by 2/2nd Londons from INDIAN VILLAGE; Bn in Bde Reserve at 10.P.M.	
"	24-4-15		Quiet day, slight shelling.	
"			Bn was relieved and marched to Billets at HARISOIRS, about 6 miles.	
HARISOIRS	25-4-15		Bn rested	
"	26-4-15			
"	27-4-15		Coy training etc, Lecture at Divl H.Q. by G.O.C. Divn. On attack.	
"	28-4-15		Coy training etc, Lt. Minstall returned to duty.	
"	29-4-15		Bn practised the ASSAULT on the prepared ground. 1 man stuck with a bayonet.	
"	30-4-15		Practice Assault again, to satisfaction of G.O.C. G.O.C. 1st Divn inspected Bn in afternoon.	

30/4/15

C.J. ——— Capt.
Capt.
for O.C. 4th R.W.F.
to O.C. 4th R.W.F.

1577 Wt.W10791/1773 500,000 1/15 D.D.&L. A.D.S.S./Forms/C. 2118.

3rd Infantry Brigade.
1st Division.

4th BATTN. ROYAL WELCH FUSILIERS.

M A Y

1 9 1 5

Army Form C. 2118.

WAR DIARY
or
INTELLIGENCE SUMMARY.
(Erase heading not required.)

Instructions regarding War Diaries and Intelligence Summaries are contained in F. S. Regs., Part II. and the Staff Manual respectively. Title pages will be prepared in manuscript.

Place	Date	Hour	Summary of Events and Information	Remarks and references to Appendices
HARISOIRS	May 1st		B⁺ at rest at HARISOIRS, men washed clothing etc.	
"	2nd		at rest, ordinary training, football etc, sports.	
"	3rd		— Ditto. —	
"	4th		— Ditto. —	
"	5th		— Ditto. —	
"	6th		B⁺ moved to HINGES.	
HINGES	7th		B⁺ warned for an attack. Packs were stored etc. B⁺ started for the rendezvous at 6.30 P.M. but at 7.30 P.M. when on march was ordered to return to billets.	
"	8th		B⁺ was ordered to rendezvous again & marched at 6.30 P.M. to a position in rear of RUE-de-Bois where assault on German trenches in morning was to take place.	
RUE-de-Bois	9th	5 a.m.	Artillery Bombardment began & at 5.30 A.M. intense bombardment, at 5.40 A.M. assault was delivered, B⁺ acting as "mopping B⁺" to the Brigade	

WAR DIARY
or
INTELLIGENCE SUMMARY.
(Erase heading not required.)

Army Form C. 2118.

Place	Date	Hour	Summary of Events and Information	Remarks and references to Appendices
Rue-M- Bois	May 9th		Assault failed & Bn lost following casualties in advancing from the Breastworks to front line Breastworks.	support
			Lieut-Col F.C. France-Hayhurst. Killed.	
			Capt. J. Ronie Evans Died of wounds	
			Lieut B. Croom-Johnson Killed.	
			2nd Lieut J.C. Hazledene Killed.	
			Lieut M. Pern R.A.M.C. (attached) Killed.	
			2nd Lieut R. Richards wounded	
			65 other ranks Killed, wounded & missing.	
		3.30 pm	Brigade were detailed for 2nd assault 2 Coy of Bn. were again detailed for "mopping up" & 2 coys attached to 23rd Coy R.E.	
		4.P.M	Assault was again delivered & one more failed owing to M.G.uns etc. The 2 Coys reached as far as front Breastworks, using Com. Trench & Bn only suffered very slightly.	
		6.30 pm	Part of Brigade was withdrawn & Bn ordered to march to billets when Bn billeted at HARISOIR for the night.	

Army Form C. 2118.

WAR DIARY
or
INTELLIGENCE SUMMARY.
(Erase heading not required.)

Place	Date	Hour	Summary of Events and Information	Remarks and references to Appendices
HARISOIR	May 10th		Bn. changed billets to LONG CORNET. Draft of 17 men rejoined Bn. for duty. Bn. as part of the 3rd Bde. was highly complimented on its bearing in the action on the 9th inst. both by G.O.C Div. & Bde.	
LONG CORNET	11th		Bn. moved into Reserve trenches at CUINCHY. 2nd Lt. Clayton to Hos. sick.	
CUINCHY	12th		Bn. still at CUINCHY.	
"	13th	6.AM	Bn. was relieved by 21st LONDON REGT. at 6.AM. & marched to billets at ANNEQUIN, at 4.P.M. Bn. relieved 141st T. Regt. French Inf. 58th Divn in french trenches.	A/23
"	14th		Bn. occupied the same section.	
"	15th		In trenches, heavy fig[hting] by French on Right & British on Left.	
"	16th		2/Lt. Ward & Draft of 50 men arrived.	
"	17th		Rained, otherwise situation same.	
"	18th		Cold & Damp situation same!	
"	19th		— Ditto —	

WAR DIARY
or
INTELLIGENCE SUMMARY.
(Erase heading not required.)

Army Form C. 2118.

Place	Date	Hour	Summary of Events and Information	Remarks and references to Appendices
CUINCHY	20th		Relieved by 9th Liverpool. H.Q. shelled in morning. Bn. marched to Beuvry.	
BEUVRY	21st		Bn. cleaning on relief to BEUVRY.	1/23
			Bn. ordered to relieve 24th London Regt. in ANNEQUIN, as Brigade Reserve, heavy shelling all day by our guns to support Canadians.	
ANNEQUIN	22nd		Quiet day, Pte Clay in return to duty.	
	23rd		Quiet day, Church Service by Padre, issue of clean clothing.	
	24th		Quiet day.	
	25th		Bn. relieved S.W.B. as Reserve to "A" Sect at TOURBIERE [Canadians made an attack in afternoon on our left, our guns in rear supporting.]	
TOURBIERE	26th		At pm 25th Lt C O'Darius went to 1st Corps for duty.	
	27th		Quiet day.	
	28th		Quiet day reconnoitred 1st line Trenches with a view to relief, relief cancelled. Heavy shelling in front line.	

WAR DIARY
or
INTELLIGENCE SUMMARY.
(Erase heading not required.)

Army Form C. 2118.

Instructions regarding War Diaries and Intelligence Summaries are contained in F. S. Regs., Part II. and the Staff Manual respectively. Title pages will be prepared in manuscript.

Place	Date	Hour	Summary of Events and Information	Remarks and references to Appendices
TOURBIERES VERQUIGNEOL	29th		Bn. moved as part of Brigade to LABOURSE & VERQUIGNEOL where they were billeted in Bivs. Reserve.	
"	30th		Sunday, Service in the field by the Padre, quiet day.	
"	31st		Quiet day, Bn. was issued to Shift-Billets.	

C. Bernard Colter
Lt. Col. Comdg.
1st R. Inniskilling Fus.

Ex. 3
31=5=15

3rd Infantry Brigade.
1st Division.

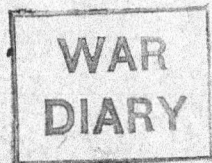

4th BATTN. ROYAL WELCH FUSILIERS.

J U N E

1 9 1 5

WAR DIARY
or
INTELLIGENCE SUMMARY.

Army Form C. 2118.

(Erase heading not required.)

Instructions regarding War Diaries and Intelligence Summaries are contained in F. S. Regs., Part II. and the Staff Manual respectively. Title pages will be prepared in manuscript.

Place	Date	Hour	Summary of Events and Information	Remarks and references to Appendices
VERQUIGNEUL	June 1st		B⁵ inspected by Corps Commander, who commented on the healthy appearance & good turn out of the men; at 10 P.M. B⁵ was relieved by 21st London Regt & marched to LABEUVIERE arriving at 2-30 P.M. when it was billeted.	
LABEUVRIERE	" 2nd		B⁵ at rest.	
"	" 3rd		B⁵ at rest. Training continued etc.	
CUINCHY	" 4th		B⁵ marched to CUINCHY & took over Sub-Sect A 3 from 5th Bn Sussex Regt. A long & tiring march. 2 men wounded.	
"	" 5th		Day fairly quiet, a certain number of Rifle Grenades & mortar Bombs sent over by the enemy. 1 man killed. 4 men wounded.	
"	" 6th		Quiet day, several R.A. & 1st Bde Officers came to our front line. during day several mortar bombs were sent over, on knocking our M. Gun, no damage but 1 man wounded. During the night several Grenades sent over. Lt. N. Hugh Jones, M. Gun Officer wounded. 1 man killed. 4 men wounded.	
"	" 7th		Quiet day, were handing etc B⁵ relieved at 6. P.M. by 2nd R.M.F. & took our supports at GLASGOW ROAD, CUINCHY DEFENCES, MAISON ROUGE & CAMBRIN.	

WAR DIARY
or
INTELLIGENCE SUMMARY.
(Erase heading not required.)

Army Form C. 2118.

Instructions regarding War Diaries and Intelligence Summaries are contained in F.S. Regs., Part II. and the Staff Manual respectively. Title pages will be prepared in manuscript.

Place	Date	Hour	Summary of Events and Information	Remarks and references to Appendices
CUINCHY	June 8th		Quiet day, Plan of rest. 3 men wounded.	
"	" 9		Quiet day, a certain amount of shelling, no damage.	
"	" 10		Quiet day. Bn was relieved by 2nd Coldstream Guards and marched to billets at FAUBOURG D'ARRAS, BETHUNE.	
BETHUNE	" 11		at rest: huge means to hospital sick.	
"	" 12		at rest: training, usual routine exercise on. Part of Bn went to concert organised by Bde.	
"	" 13		Sunday. Bn bathed between 6 A.M & 9 A.M. at Swimming Baths. Divine Service - C.O. & in station. Nonconformists at College.	
"	" 14		Routine training in morning. Boxing contests in afternoon + evening.	
"	" 15		Usual training.	
"	" 16		Usual training.	
"	" 17		Lieut-Col S. Pereira C.M.G. D.S.O. took over command of Bn.	
"	" 18		Usual training. 2nd Lieut A. Gurney 1st Grenadier Regt appointed A/adjt pending confirmation. Bn won 3rd Bde swimming race.	

WAR DIARY
or
INTELLIGENCE SUMMARY.
(Erase heading not required.)

Army Form C. 2118.

Instructions regarding War Diaries and Intelligence Summaries are contained in F. S. Regs., Part II. and the Staff Manual respectively. Title pages will be prepared in manuscript.

Place	Date	Hour	Summary of Events and Information	Remarks and references to Appendices
BETHUNE	June 19		Moral Training. Brigade Sports.	
"	" 20		Usual Training.	
"	" 21		Do.	
"	" 22		Do.	
"	" 23		Do.	
"	" 24		Do.	
"	" 25		Battalion moved with the Brigade from FABOURG D'ARRAS, BETHUNE to billets at AUCHEL.	
AUCHEL	" 26		Brigade Route march.	
"	" 27		Divine Service & Training in bombing attack.	
"	" 28		The Battalion moved to NOYELLES les VERMELLES & relieved H.L.I. + remained in Brigade reserve.	
NOYELLES les VERMELLES	" 29		Battalion in Brigade Reserve at NOYELLES les VERMELLES	
"	" 30		Do.	

30/6/15

G. Beevor Lieut Col
Comm'g 4. R.W.F.

3rd Infantry Brigade.

1st Division.

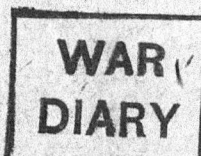

4th BATTN. ROYAL WELCH FUSILIERS.

J U L Y

1 9 1 5

Army Form C. 2118

WAR DIARY
or
INTELLIGENCE SUMMARY.
(Erase heading not required.)

Instructions regarding War Diaries and Intelligence Summaries are contained in F. S. Regs., Part II. and the Staff Manual respectively. Title pages will be prepared in manuscript.

Place	Date	Hour	Summary of Events and Information	Remarks and references to Appendices
NOYELLES LES VERMELLES	1/7/15		Battalion in Brigade Reserve at NOYELLES LES VERMELLES	
VERMELLES	2/7/15		The Battalion relieved 2nd Royal Munsters in Trenches in the firing line sect Y2.	
"	3/7/15		E. of VERMELLES. An occupation of Trenches at Y 2.	
"	4/7/15		— Ditto —	
"	5/7/15		The Battalion was relieved by the Cameron Highlanders at 10. P.M. & marched to billets at FOUQUEREUIL.	
FOUQUEREUIL	6/7/15		Rest Day.	
"	7/7/15		Usual Training.	
"	8/7/15		The 3rd Brigade lined the HESDIGNEUL — BETHUNE ROAD on the occasion of the visit of Earl Kitchener who passed through the ranks of the troops drawn up on both sides of the road. Earl Kitchener expressed his admiration at the smart manner in which The Brigade was turned out & the excellent appearance of the troops.	
"	9/7/15		Usual Training	
"	10/7/15		— Ditto —	

Army Form C. 2118.

WAR DIARY
or
INTELLIGENCE SUMMARY.
(Erase heading not required.)

Instructions regarding War Diaries and Intelligence Summaries are contained in F. S. Regs., Part II. and the Staff Manual respectively. Title pages will be prepared in manuscript.

Place	Date	Hour	Summary of Events and Information	Remarks and references to Appendices
FOUQUEREUIL	11/2/15		Usual Training.	
"	12/2/15		— Ditto —	
"	13/2/15		The Battalion moved into front line trenches, in relief of 3rd Battalion Coldstream Guards about 1.000 yards S.E of CUINCHY. These trenches were about 80 to 120 yards from the enemy.	
CUINCHY	14/2/15		& occupation of these trenches.	
"	15/2/15		— Ditto —	
"	16/2/15		— Ditto —	
"	17/2/15		— Ditto —	
"	18/2/15		— Ditto —	
"			During the occupation of these trenches Bombing Duels took place daily & the supremacy generally held by the 3rd Coldstream Guards was maintained by The Battalion.	
"	19/2/15		The Battalion was relieved at about 6.P.M from the front line by the 1st Bn. Scots & S.W Bs. & moved into reserve trenches & Bomb groups at MAISON ROUGE & CAMBRIN.	

1577 Wt.W10791/1773 500,000 1/15 D. D. & L. A.D.S.S./Forms/C. 2118.

WAR DIARY
or
INTELLIGENCE SUMMARY.

Army Form C. 2118.

Place	Date	Hour	Summary of Events and Information	Remarks and references to Appendices
CAMBRIN	20/8/15		4 Brigade Reserve at MAISON ROUGE & CAMBRIN.	
"	21/8/15		Ditto —	
"	22/8/15		Ditto —	
"	23/8/15		Ditto —	
"	24/8/15		Ditto —	
			During the period the Battalion was in Brigade Reserve good work on new trenches was carried out by large working parties. The Battalion was relieved by the London Scottish & marched to billets	
"	25/8/15		at VERQUIN.	
VERQUIN	26/8/15		Usual Training.	
"	27/8/15		— Ditto —	
"	28/8/15		— Ditto —	
"	29/8/15		— Ditto —	
"	30/8/15		— Ditto —	
"	31/8/15		The Battalion to NOYELLES — LES — VERMELLES in relief of the Northampton Regiment & remained in Brigade Reserve.	

A Brown Lieut Col
Command 4: R.W. Fus

3rd Infantry Brigade.

1st Division.

(Became Pioneers to 47th Division 1.9.15.)

4th BATTN. ROYAL WELCH FUSILIERS.

A U G U S T

1 9 1 5

WAR DIARY
or
INTELLIGENCE SUMMARY.

(Erase heading not required.)

Army Form C. 2118.

Place	Date	Hour	Summary of Events and Information	Remarks and references to Appendices
NOYELLES-LES-VERMELLES	1.8.15		In Brigade Reserve at NOYELLES-LES-VERMELLES	
"	2.8.15		——— Ditto ———	
"	3.8.15		——— Ditto ———	
"	4.8.15		——— Ditto ———	
"	5.8.15		——— Ditto ———	
VERMELLES	6.8.15		The Battalion relieved the 2nd Battn R. Munster Fus. in front line trenches Y2.	
"	7.8.15		In occupation of these trenches	
"	8.8.15		——— Ditto ———	
"	9.8.15		——— Ditto ———	
"	10.8.15		——— Ditto ———	
"	11.8.15		——— Ditto ———	
			During the occupation of this section (Y2) the men of the Battalion did excellent work in constructing bomb-proof shelters. Brigadier-Gen Davies commanding 3rd Bde spoke very highly of the work performed.	
	12.8.15		The Battalion was relieved by 1st Bn London Scottish & moved into BRETT RIVER CAMP (FOUQUEREIL)	

Army Form C. 2118.

WAR DIARY
or
INTELLIGENCE SUMMARY.
(Erase heading not required.)

Instructions regarding War Diaries and Intelligence Summaries are contained in F. S. Regs., Part II and the Staff Manual respectively. Title pages will be prepared in manuscript.

Place	Date	Hour	Summary of Events and Information	Remarks and references to Appendices
BRETT RIVER CAMP	13/8/15		Battalion at rest BRETT RIVER CAMP.	
"	14/8/15		Ditto	
"	15/8/15		Ditto	
"	16/8/15		Ditto	
"	17/8/15		Ditto	
"	18/8/15		While at BRETT RIVER CAMP the Battn. did good work in improving the sanitary condition of the CAMP, and many roads were made. The Battalion moved to ANNEQUIN in relief of the 5th Battn. Sussex & remained there in Brigade Reserve.	
ANNEQUIN	19/8/15		In Brigade Reserve. Working parties found for work under 26th Coy. R.E.	
"	20/8/15		Ditto	
"	21/8/15		Ditto	
"	22/8/15		Ditto	

WAR DIARY
or
INTELLIGENCE SUMMARY.

(Erase heading not required.)

Army Form C. 2118

Instructions regarding War Diaries and Intelligence Summaries are contained in F. S. Regs., Part II. and the Staff Manual respectively. Title pages will be prepared in manuscript.

Place	Date	Hour	Summary of Events and Information	Remarks and references to Appendices
CAMBRIN	22/8/15		The Battn. moved into the front line trenches in relief of 2 Coys of 1st Battn. Gloucester Regt. in Section Z.1 (CAMBRIN) 2nd Lieut R.P. Davies (late Regt Sergt-Major of the Battn.) gazetted, posted and joined the Battn.	
"	23/8/15		In occupation of trenches, Z.1. quiet day	
"	24/8/15		Ditto quiet day	
"	25/8/15		Ditto	
			Lieut A.E. Picton Davies 2nd Battn. R.W.F. joined for duty	
			2nd Lieut J.J. Wolff 3rd " " "	
			" M.J. Wilson " " "	
			" D.E. Gibbins " " "	
			" J.R. Owen " " "	
"	26/8/15		In occupation of trenches Z.1. quiet day	
"	27/8/15		Ditto Enemy shelled support line with H.E., our artillery retaliated on Enemys Support trenches Battn. relieved by R. Munster Fus. & moved into Brigade Reserve situated as under. C Coy. SIMS' KEEP, ARTHUR'S KEEP and RUSSELL'S KEEP A + B Coys. MAISON ROUGE & D Coy to CAMBRIN.	

Army Form C. 2118

WAR DIARY
or
INTELLIGENCE SUMMARY.
(Erase heading not required.)

Instructions regarding War Diaries and Intelligence Summaries are contained in F. S. Regs., Part II. and the Staff Manual respectively. Title pages will be prepared in manuscript.

Place	Date	Hour	Summary of Events and Information	Remarks and references to Appendices
MAISON ROUGE CAMBRIN	28/8/15		In Brigade Reserve	
"	29/8/15		Ditto	
"	30/8/15		Ditto	
"	31/8/15		Ditto	

Greens Lieut Colonel.
Commanding 4th Bn. R. W. Fus.

www.ingramcontent.com/pod-product-compliance
Lightning Source LLC
Chambersburg PA
CBHW081447160426
43193CB00013B/2399